The Art Institute of Chicago

The Trading Room

Louis Sullivan and The Chicago Stock Exchange

The Art Institute of Chicago

John Vinci
With a foreword by Pauline Saliga

**The
Trading
Room**
Louis
Sullivan
and
The
Chicago
Stock
Exchange

Front cover:
Top: Detail of stencil border above the paneling on the north, east, and south walls of Adler and Sullivan's Chicago Stock Exchange Trading Room. The canvas stencil is painted with twenty-eight colors (Hedrich Blessing). Inset: View of the reconstructed Trading Room at The Art Institute of Chicago, 1983 (Bob Thall).

Frontispiece: Engraving of the Chicago Stock Exchange Building that was used as the illustration on a directory of the Stock Exchange.

Richard Nickel, 1928—1972

Many of the photographs in this book are the work of the architectural photographer Richard Nickel. A 1954 graduate of the Institute of Design, Illinois Institute of Technology, Nickel went on to receive a Master of Photography degree in 1957. His master's thesis, *A Photographic Documentation of Adler and Sullivan*, resulted in the discovery of many projects by the firm that were previously unknown. When the opportunity came to work on dismantling the Trading Room for preservation at the Art Institute, Richard Nickel agreed to join the effort and make the necessary photographs. On January 31, 1972, the salvaging of the Trading Room was completed. On April 13, 1972, Nickel went into the partially wrecked building and was not seen again. His body was found four weeks later in the debris.

Acknowledgments

The editor would like to thank Robert V. Sharp, Associate Editor in the Art Institute's Publications Department, whose encouragement during this project was unfailing. Kathy Houck, Cris Ligenza, Amy E. Linenthal, and Susan A. Snodgrass, also of the Publications Department, assisted in preparing and checking the manuscript. Thanks also to Michelle Klarich, Robert Lifson, and Lorri Zipperer of the Department of Photographic Services, and to Nancy Galles of the Department of Graphic Services. For the notable contributions made by those outside of the Art Institute's staff, special thanks are due. Ward A. Miller's cooperation was invaluable as he worked with the author and editor in locating photographs in the Richard Nickel archive. Book designer Rhonda Taira gave this volume its fresh and elegant visual qualities. The 1977 edition of this book, from which the current one evolved, was realized through the efforts of Kathleen Roy Cummings and David Norris; Irma Strauss contributed information about Sullivan's stencils. Finally, the Art Institute is grateful to W. R. Hasbrouck, Tim Samuelson, and Powell's Bookstore, whose loans of objects to be photographed enhanced the book's illustrations.

Susan F. Rossen, Executive Director of Publications
Edited by Peter M. Junker, Assistant Editor
Katherine A. Houck, Production Manager
Designed and typeset in Bodoni and Helvetica Condensed by Ligature Inc., Chicago, Illinois; pages composed on the Apple® Macintosh™ desktop publishing system.
Printed by Eastern Press, New Haven, Connecticut, on Warren Lustro Offset Enamel Dull.

Contents

Foreword

If one had to choose for preservation an architectural interior of unequaled beauty that represented ideas formative to the course of modern architecture, the Trading Room from the Chicago Stock Exchange Building would top one's list. Despite numerous obstacles that nearly led to the total destruction of the Trading Room when the Stock Exchange Building was demolished in 1972, the exquisite room from Adler and Sullivan's celebrated Chicago School office building has been preserved and reconstructed at The Art Institute of Chicago.

1. An illustration of the Trading Room from Harper's Weekly *(Jan. 12, 1895) indicates the national attention the room received.*

From the time of its completion in 1894 until its demolition in 1972, the Chicago Stock Exchange Building stood as an eloquent example of the contributions of Dankmar Adler and Louis H. Sullivan to the formation of the tall, metal-framed commercial building. The earliest metal-framed "skyscrapers" had begun to appear in Chicago nearly a decade before Adler and Sullivan received the Stock Exchange commission, but architects had continued to struggle with finding an appropriate architectural form for this unprecedented building type. The versatile technical skills of Dankmar Adler and the philosophically influenced architectural ideals of Louis H. Sullivan established precedents that addressed the interrelated functional and aesthetic aspects of the tall building. In the Stock Exchange, the architects fully integrated structure and function with creative architectural forms and unparalleled ornamental detailing, demonstrating the principles of what Sullivan called "organic architecture," and exemplifying his famous dictum "form follows function."

In addressing the problems of designing this tall office building, the architects gave the exterior a two-story arcade at the second and third floors, representing the cubic volume of the double-height Trading Room within, and distinguishing it as a specialized segment of the building. The architects interrupted the regular grid of the steel frame to accommodate the Trading Room, and they provided the building with a skin of plastic materials—terracotta on the exterior and plaster and stencils on the interior. The skin, enlivened by alternating passages of foliate ornament, projecting moldings and profiles, and flat planes, was subordinated to the structure, and also served to reflect the building's commercial function by emphasizing its internal divisions.

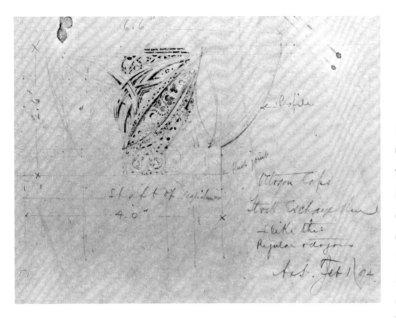

2. Detail of Louis H. Sullivan's drawing, dated February 1, 1894, for the four main column capitals in the Trading Room.

The aspect that distinguished the Chicago Stock Exchange from Adler and Sullivan's other office buildings was undoubtedly its exquisite, two-story Trading Room, located on the second and third floors. The Stock Exchange presented a unique opportunity because one of its functional requirements was a large, unobstructed room to be devoted to trading. Adler and Sullivan obliged by designing a truss system that diverted the weight of the fourth through the thirteenth floors around the open volume of the Trading Room, and by covering the trusses and interior of the room with some of their most refined and poetic architectural ornament.

In his seminal article "Architecture and Ornament" (1892), Sullivan wrote that architectural ornament should be organic, deriving its form from nature. The Trading Room's opulent ornament and verdant color scheme created the impression of a pastoral respite in the heart of an office building, reflecting Sullivan's romantic temperament and his enduring love of nature. When one enters the Trading Room, one's eyes are immediately drawn to the ceiling and upper portion of the room, which are stenciled in six different ornamental patterns in fifty-seven shades of green, yellow, gold, rust, brown, and blue. The ornamental stencils are permutations on a theme in both pattern and color sequence. They combine complex variations of geometric forms, such as interlocking circles, ovals, diamonds, and rotated squares, to create dense patterns that lie somewhere between geometric precision and organic effusion.

The perimeter of the Trading Room ceiling is bounded by art-glass skylights. The already rich colors of the room shift subtly as the light changes at different times and under different weather conditions. The result is an aura not usually associated with an office building: the combination of natural light and color gives the room the restorative and protean qualities of a green and golden meadow.

Despite the unquestionable importance of the Chicago Stock Exchange as an example of the development of modern architecture, in 1971 its owners decided to demolish it because they considered it "economically unviable." The threat of demolition prompted public outrage that was followed by a preservation battle of proportions unprecedented in Chicago.

3. One of the four main columns with gilded-plaster capitals after reconstruction of the Trading Room, 1977. A section of the room's art-glass skylights and parts of three different stencils and three decorated moldings are also visible.

4. View of the Chicago Stock Exchange Building from the east, c. 1929. The Exchange had moved three blocks south to Burnham and Root's Rookery Building (209 South LaSalle) in 1908, and Adler and Sullivan's building was later known familiarly as the "Old Stock Exchange," or, formally, by its address, 30 North LaSalle.

Many local and national architectural organizations, such as the Landmarks Preservation Council, the Chicago Chapter of the American Institute of Architects, and the Society of Architectural Historians, fought a bitter battle to save the building. They proposed options for restoring and preserving it. They wrote impassioned pleas to the City Council and Mayor Richard J. Daley urging them to grant landmark status to the building under the newly defined legal protection of the Commission on Chicago Historical and Architectural Landmarks. They took the matter to court. They picketed in front of the building (fig. 5).

The editorial pages and columns of Chicago's daily newspapers underscored the barbarity of demolishing this important element of America's architectural heritage (figs. 49, 50). In his typically wry style, Mike Royko commented on the sad state of affairs in his *Chicago Daily News* column:

I figure that anybody who tries to save landmarks in Chicago is goofy enough to preach celibacy in a Playboy Club or nonviolence to Dick Butkus. . . . You would think that if there was one architect the City Council would honor, it would be Louis Sullivan. . . . He didn't create the modern skyscraper in New York, or Paris, or London, he did it here. Outside of Al Capone, who created the modern syndicate, Sullivan is one of our few original thinkers.

In a more sober commentary, architecture critic Ada Louis Huxtable wrote in retrospect in the *New York Times* of April 6, 1975, "Critics and preservationists bled profusely in print before it came down. . . . Arguments about quality, style, and the Chicago heritage were to no avail." After public hearings, the City Council voted against landmark designation for the Stock Exchange Building, which assured its demolition.

5. *One of many protests to save Adler and Sullivan's Stock Exchange Building. There was public concern that, as a Chicago Sun-Times editorialist put it (Oct. 5, 1970), "one by one our great buildings have been knocked to smithereens."*

Once it was clear that the building would not survive intact, several cultural institutions expressed their interest in preserving parts of the building. The City of Chicago stepped in to assist with complex negotiations among the cultural institutions, building owners, developers, and wrecking company to document and preserve important aspects of the building. At the time, some critics questioned the value of parceling the building up and donating its parts to museums. But as Huxtable wrote in the December 26, 1971 issue of the *New York Times*, although the solution was imperfect, it did prevent the total loss of this aspect of our architectural heritage:

Using building fragments applied to other buildings or set up in galleries is a bad joke. The farce we go through of destroying a city's living substance and then stashing dead tokens in alien settings is the kind of false conscience balm that can only be called stupid, willful or otherwise. But when a building is being wrecked, arguments about *in situ* preservation become pointless. Then one is forced to deal with its parts as artifacts rather than suffer total esthetic loss.

6. View of the seventy-seven-year-old Chicago Stock Exchange Building (30 North LaSalle), 1971. The scaffolding for the building's demolition can be seen going up at left.

The Art Institute of Chicago was offered first choice of fragments, and the institution decided that, instead of taking numerous small artifacts, it would concentrate its efforts on reconstructing the magnificent Trading Room. Soon after the Art Institute commenced its Centennial Project, which would include the construction of a new wing to house the Trading Room and the School of the Art Institute, the City of Chicago donated the Stock Exchange's LaSalle Street entrance arch to the museum. The Art Institute also purchased and received gifts of several smaller fragments from the building, including a bank of cast-iron elevator enclosure grilles and numerous other terracotta, cast-iron, and copper elements from the interior and exterior. Other institutions that also acquired fragments from the building included the University of Illinois at Chicago, Southern Illinois University at Edwardsville, the Chicago Historical Society, and the Metropolitan Museum of Art in New York.

To acquire the decorative plaster and stenciled canvas features that comprised the Trading Room, the Art Institute's Trustees assigned funds to pay for their careful removal. The artifacts were donated by the owners of the Stock Exchange Building, the City of Chicago, and Three Oaks Wrecking Company. Generous gifts from Mrs. Eugene A. Davidson and the Graham Foundation for Advanced Studies in the Fine Arts allowed the Art Institute to purchase the Trading Room's art-glass windows and iron mullions from the demolition company.

The architectural firm of John Vinci and Lawrence Kenny, which had supervised the removal of the fragments, devised a plan to reconstruct the Trading Room skillfully and accurately. Research was crucial to insure the precise reconstruction of the room's features, many of which had been removed long before. The research of Sullivan expert Tim Samuelson proved invaluable, and authoritative analysis of the stencils and their re-creation was skillfully overseen by Robert A. Furhoff.

Through the generosity of the Walter E. Heller Foundation and its president, Mrs. Edwin J. DeCosta, the Trading Room grew from a collection of architectural fragments to a magnificent reconstructed room.

The Heller Foundation also funded the reconstruction of the Stock Exchange's LaSalle Street entrance arch, which was reassembled outdoors at Monroe Street and Columbus Drive, adjacent to the newly opened East Wing, renamed the Arthur Rubloff Building in 1985 (fig. 58). With the cooperation of Skidmore, Owings and Merrill, the Art Institute staff, and the Reed Illinois Corporation, the reconstruction was smoothly executed.

When all is said and done, a great debt continues to be owed to Mrs. Edwin J. DeCosta, whose enthusiasm for architecture is undiminished more than ten years after the reconstruction of the Trading Room, and who still supports the high standards necessary to preserve Chicago's internationally renowned architectural heritage.

The Trading Room now is overseen by the Department of Architecture at the Art Institute which, in 1986, organized "Fragments of Chicago's Past," a permanent exhibition of terracotta, plaster, cast-iron, and glass fragments from other significant Chicago buildings that have been altered or demolished. It is our hope that these poignant reminders of our lost architectural heritage will encourage the preservation of our remaining treasures.

Pauline Saliga
Assistant Curator of Architecture
The Art Institute of Chicago

For nearly eighty years the Chicago Stock Exchange Building stood at the southwest corner of LaSalle and Washington streets. Its light buff-colored terracotta facade seemed to loom forward and upward where LaSalle Street narrowed to the south.

In the 1830s, the corner had been the home-site of pioneer merchant P. F. W. Peck, but it was soon redeveloped for commercial purposes as the city rapidly expanded. After the Chicago Fire of 1871, the site was developed with two five-story office buildings, but the phenomenal growth of the city and the introduction of technologies that gave birth to the highrise soon rendered these buildings obsolete. By the early 1890s, Ferdinand W. Peck, a son of the original settler, began exploring the possibilities of developing the corner with a more profitable highrise.

7. View of the LaSalle Street entrance arch of the Stock Exchange Building, 1894. Two medallions commemorate the site of the homestead of P. F. W. Peck, whose son commissioned Adler and Sullivan's building. The claim that the Peck home was Chicago's first brick building was later disproved.

The Chicago Stock Exchange Building

Peck was involved in the city's civic activities and was one of the earliest patrons of the architectural firm of Adler and Sullivan. From him came such major commissions as the temporary opera festival theater, erected in 1885 within the lakefront Exposition Building on the site where The Art Institute of Chicago now stands, and the Auditorium Building, a combination theater, hotel, and office building at Michigan Avenue and Congress Street. Through his patronage, Peck was instrumental in bringing the innovative work of Dankmar Adler and Louis H. Sullivan to international prominence.

Peck awarded the commission for the new office building at Washington and LaSalle streets to Adler and Sullivan, and work was begun in early 1893 on demolishing the existing buildings on the site. The new commission stipulated a metal-framed, thirteen-story office building. It was decided to incorporate a major space into the structure for use as a trading room by the growing Chicago Stock Exchange, and, thus, to encourage office tenancy by brokerage firms and related professions. The Stock Exchange was given a fifteen-year, rent-free lease, and the building took its name.

The design of the building revealed Sullivan's famed dictum "form follows function." He codified this idea three years later in his essay "The Tall Office Building Artistically Considered" (1896):

Beginning with the first story, we give this a main entrance that attracts the eye to its location, and the remainder of the story we treat in a more or less liberal, expansive, sumptuous way—a way based exactly on the practical necessities, but expressed with a sentiment of largeness and freedom. The second story we treat in a similar way, but usually with milder pretension. Above this, throughout the indefinite number of typical office tiers, we take our cue from the individual cell, which requires a window with its separating pier, its sill and lintel, and we, without more ado, make them look all alike because they are all alike. This brings us to the attic, which, having no division into office-cells, and no special requirement for lighting, gives us the power to show by means of its broad expanse of wall, and its dominating weight and character, that which is the fact—namely that the series of office tiers has come definitely to an end.

These principles, slightly modified, were used in the Chicago Stock Exchange Building. The great terracotta arch called attention to the entrance, and the remainder of the ground floor, occupied by shops, was treated straightforwardly. The second-floor facade was not handled in a similar way, but combined with that of the third floor into a richly ornamented arcade, to reflect the presence of the Trading Room and an adjacent banking space (fig. 12). The typical office tiers were varied by alternating flat planes of "Chicago windows" — fixed panes of glass flanked by narrow, movable windows — with three-sided projecting bays. The attic story, concealed by an ornamental cornice, brought the building to a definite and dramatic conclusion.

Construction, begun in the summer of 1893, was completed the following spring. Special circumstances required that caisson foundations be designed by bridge engineer William Sooy Smith to support the west wall. This first use of such foundations in Chicago avoided the damage that might have occurred to newspaper presses in the adjacent Chicago Herald Building had traditional pilings been driven in the area. Although the original cost of the building was estimated at $1,800,000, the financial panic of 1893 allowed bids to come in lower. Construction was slowed by strikes and interrupted by delays in receiving materials, but the final cost amounted to $1,131,555.

9. View of the "Golden Door," the main entrance to Adler and Sullivan's Transportation Building at the 1893 World's Columbian Exposition. The decorated, semicircular arch was a design element that appeared in many Sullivan projects.

10. Detail of the LaSalle Street entrance arch of the building showing the south medallion. The Peck family residence, which originally occupied the site, is depicted.

At the LaSalle Street entrance to the building, the architects elected to design a large terra-cotta portal, three bays wide and two stories high (approximately 40 by 30 feet), framing a semicircular arch (fig. 7). This design element had been used in other Adler and Sullivan projects; the most prominent was the entrance to their Transportation Building for the World's Columbian Exposition in 1893. Referred to as the "Golden Door," the great wood-framed arch covered in gilded and polychromed plaster (fig. 9) was one of the most admired features of the World's Fair.

11. Detail of the LaSalle Street entrance arch of the building showing the second north medallion.

12. Detail of the exterior arcade above the second and third floors of the building. The arcade visually distinguished the two floors, suggesting the location and functional inter-relationship of the Trading Room and banking space within.

In the Stock Exchange Building, the portal and its arch served two functions. Attention was called to the main entrance, and the articulation of the arch's tympanum suggested that the ground floor and second floor were functionally interrelated. At the street level, vertical divisions provided for four double doors with ornamented bronze-plated kickplates and hardware (see fig. 7). An arched transom expressed the vaulted ceiling of the entrance vestibule, and the bronze lintel above defined the level of the second or main floor. The terracotta ornament for this entrance portal has been considered among Sullivan's most brilliant designs. Incorporated in the upper spandrels of the arch are two commemorative medallions, four feet in diameter (figs. 10, 11). The left medallion depicts the house of P. F. W. Peck, the first structure on the site. The right medallion originally carried the legend "The First Brick Building Erected In Chicago Was Built Upon This Site." As the building was nearing completion, this was discovered to be untrue, and the right medallion was replaced with one bearing the date "1893," the year construction began.

*13. Louis H.
Sullivan's drawing
for the angle block in
the railing of the
second-floor main
staircase outside the
Trading Room. The
angle blocks are
visible in figure 14.*

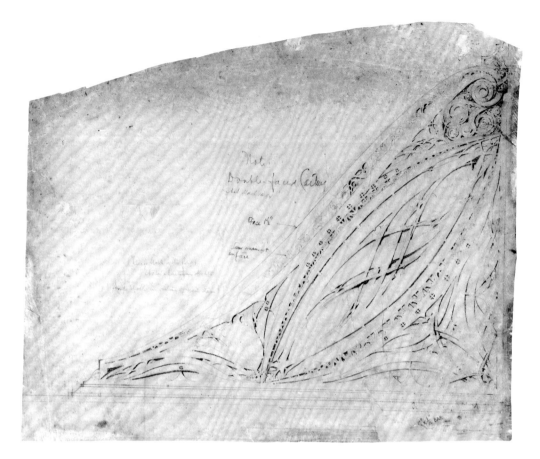

Behind the doubled entrance doors was the small vestibule spanned by a mosaic vault. Just beyond the vestibule, Sullivan enhanced the entrance hall with marble staircases on either side which met above the vestibule vault and opened to a wide landing on the second (or main) floor before ending at the third floor. The stair balustrades, with Sullivan-ornamented balusters (fig. 14), were of iron, the same material used throughout the building for the grilles enclosing the elevator shafts. On the ground and main floors these grilles were embellished with ornamental cast-iron panels and framed by cast-iron casings finished in bronze electroplate (fig. 16). (Although few of these grilles survived, the Art Institute was able to purchase one entire bank during demolition from funds provided by the Graham Foundation for Advanced Studies in the Fine Arts.)

14. (above, left) The second-floor main staircase to the south, above the LaSalle Street vestibule, 1894. The entrance to the Trading Room appears to the right. These stairs were removed during the tenancy of the Foreman Brothers' Banking Company.

15. (below, left) View of the second-floor landing, facing east toward LaSalle Street, 1894. The window at floor-level looked out from the top of the entrance arch. The entrance to the Trading Room was adjacent to the stairs at right (see floor plan, fig. 22).

A different design, employed for the elevator grilles from floors three through thirteen, combined strap iron with small iron spheres (fig. 17). Originally given a dark blue-black finish, these grilles were ornamented with cast-bronze T-plates (fig. 18) and, like the ground-floor grilles, framed by bronze-plated cast-iron casings. Examples of these assemblies entered the Art Institute's collection in the early 1960s, when they were replaced or discarded as the building was modernized.

With the Stock Exchange, Adler and Sullivan created a building that served a variety of functions while realizing an architectural system whose aspects worked as a unified whole. The Department of Architecture at the Art Institute preserves in its collection a number of fragments — kickplates, mail slots, a baluster panel, and so on — all designed and used as parts of an original, living building. The separate aesthetic merits of these fragments continue to represent the Stock Exchange's importance in the vision of Adler and Sullivan, as does the more complex and magnificent fragment, the Trading Room.

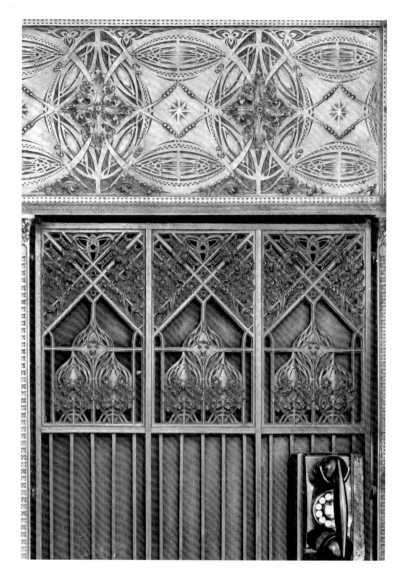

16. *Photograph of an elevator grille in the ground-floor vestibule, c. 1959. (The awkwardly installed telephone was a later addition.)*

17. *Photograph of the elevator grilles used on floors 3-13, c. 1959.*

18. *Photograph of a bronze T-plate used on the elevator grilles.*

The principal entrance to the Trading Room was on the second floor to the south of the main staircases. Upon entering, the visitor would be unexpectedly confronted by a space with a 30-foot-high ceiling, a floor area measuring 64 by 81 feet, and an upper-level, 16-foot-deep gallery running the length of the west wall.

Hailed in its day as "unexcelled in the magnificence of its appointments and decoration by any room used for like purpose in the country," the room was also innovative in its structural design.

19. Members of the Chicago Stock Exchange in the Trading Room shortly after its opening in 1894. The magnificent decoration of the room was considered remarkable for a commercial space.

The
Trading
Room

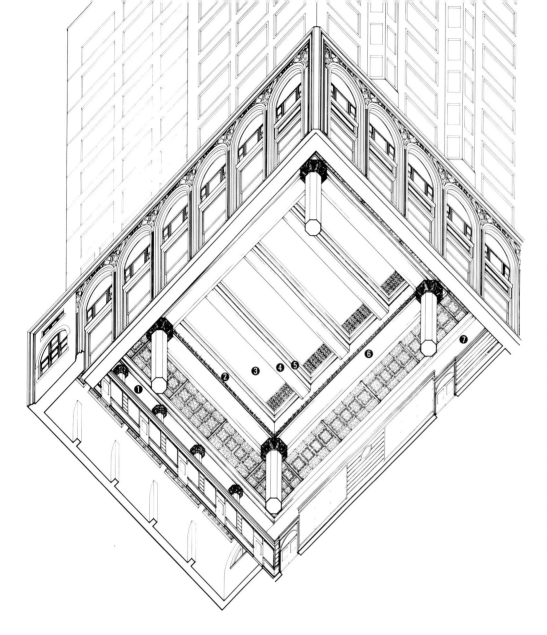

20. *Axonometric drawing of the Trading Room revealing its placement within the building (prepared by the office of John Vinci). The numbers indicate the location of the different decorative stencils illustrated in chapter three: (1) bottom of beam between Trading Room and gallery; (2) face of main trusses; (3) ceiling coffers; (4) bottom of upper beams; (5) face of upper beams; (6) bottom of main trusses; (7) north, east, and south walls above paneling.*

26   *The Trading Room*

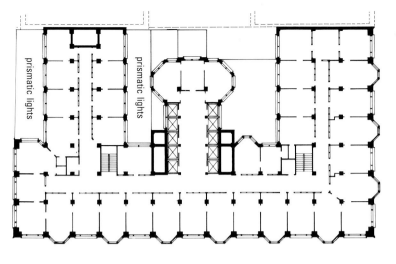

prismatic lights

prismatic lights

21. A typical floor plan for floors 4–12 of the Chicago Stock Exchange Building.

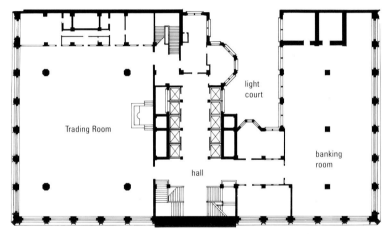

Trading Room

light court

banking room

hall

22. Second (main) floor plan of the Chicago Stock Exchange Building. The large, open space of the Trading Room was a recent innovation within a highrise.

23. Floor plan of the Trading Room, prepared by the office of John Vinci.

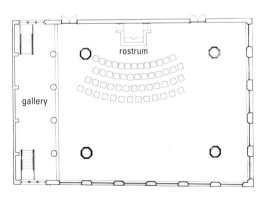

rostrum

gallery

To fulfill the client's requirement of a large, unobstructed area for a trading floor, Dankmar Adler designed a steel framing system that permitted the elimination of intermediate supports, yet carried eleven floors above.   A rectangular inverted box of steel trusses above the Trading Room's ceiling transferred the weight of the upper floors to four columns within the room's space (fig. 24).   The perimeter of the box was formed by four large trusses, each 13 ft. 6 in. deep. Three additional trusses, each 6 ft. 9 in. deep, bridged its short (40 ft. 6 in.) dimension. A coffered and stenciled plaster ceiling, while concealing the trusses, indicated their location and relative depths.

24. Tracings from Adler and Sullivan's drawings of transverse and longitudinal sections of the Trading Room, indicating the steel trusses which carried the weight of eleven floors above. The room's ornamented, coffered ceiling hid these trusses, but also signified their location and relative depths.

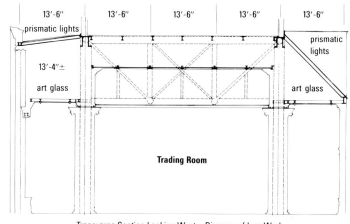

Transverse Section Looking West   Diagram of Iron Work

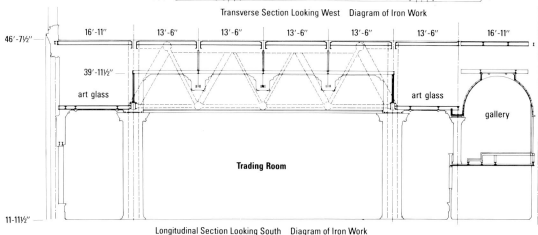

Longitudinal Section Looking South   Diagram of Iron Work

25. View to the northwest of the reconstructed Trading Room within The Art Institute of Chicago's Arthur Rubloff Building.

The development of the structural daring required to achieve a space like the Trading Room within a highrise building or a large-spanned public space can be traced through earlier Adler and Sullivan projects in Chicago: the Auditorium Building, at Michigan Avenue and Congress Street (1886–90); the now-demolished Schiller (later, Garrick) Theater, 64 West Randolph Street (1890–92); and the KAM Synagogue, 3301 South Indiana Avenue (1890–91, now Pilgrim Baptist Church).

The Michigan Avenue lobbies of the hotel incorporated into the Auditorium Building were rectangular spaces on two floors, enclosed in bearing walls, and connected by a grand staircase. Within each space, a line of five cast-iron columns sheathed in scagliola supported plaster-encased cast-iron beams (figs. 27, 28). Sullivan expressed this traditional post-and-beam construction through the manner in which he ornamented the columns and ceiling, but he wished to interrupt the column and beam spacing to accommodate the staircase and achieve a dramatic flow of architectural space between the floors (fig. 28).

26. *Photograph of the proscenium arch and vaulted ceiling in the Schiller (Garrick) Theater (now demolished) when it was used as a television studio in the 1950s. Like the coffered ceiling of the Trading Room, the theater's plaster vaults concealed the structural elements from which they were suspended while dramatically emphasizing the clear space of the room.*

Adler, to meet Sullivan's requirements, designed 33-foot trusses, spanning the stairwell openings on both floors, thereby transferring the weight of the upper floors to piers on either side of the openings.

In the Schiller Theater building, Adler and Sullivan faced the problem of carrying eight floors of offices above a 1300-seat theater. Like the Trading Room, this space was spanned by huge trusses, in this case 55 ft. long and 22 ft. 11 in. deep, which rested on masonry bearing-walls and carried the structural skeleton of the floors above. From these trusses the semicircular vaults of the theater shell hung as a thin membrane of plaster (fig. 26). Similarly, the clear-span auditorium of Adler and Sullivan's 1890–91 KAM Synagogue is flanked by large piers that support wooden trusses, which in turn support the clerestory and roof trusses from which the vaulted ceiling is hung, enclosing the volume of space between the trusses. (The idea of using an architectural shell suspended from trusses is also clearly evident in the ceilings of the Auditorium and the Schiller theaters, which functioned almost as megaphones for enlarging and projecting the human voice.)

The interior of the Trading Room was handled by Sullivan in a way similar to his treatment of the Auditorium Building lobbies and the KAM Synagogue tabernacle, in which the structure of the interior is expressed but somewhat masked. In all four, the volume of the space is articulated by beams and columns which are encased but which none-theless signify the actual structural members. The Trading Room is one of the last, and perhaps the boldest, of these interiors.

The room was illuminated by carbon-filament lamps set within a plaster frieze around the lower inside edge of the ceiling's inverted box (see fig. 25). The perimeter of the ceiling was of colored art glass, lighted from above by an ingenious system of skylights, whereby natural light filtered through the third floor lunettes in the east and south facades, and through shed roofs of prismatic glass on the north and south. The four monumental columns supporting the trusses were sheathed in scagliola, an artificial marble finish, and circled by brass sconces below the gilt-plaster capitals.

27. (right), 28. (below)
*Photographs of the
first-floor lobby with
grand staircase, 1910
(fig. 28), and second-
floor lobby, known as
the Reception Room,
c. 1890 (fig. 27), of
Adler and Sullivan's
Auditorium Hotel.
The Trading Room
was completed six
years after the
Auditorium lobbies,
and elements of its
design can be traced
to these interiors.*

A striking feature of the room was the contrast between the symmetry of the coffered ceiling and the asymmetry of the interior elevations (fig. 29). Double-hung windows in the east wall overlooked LaSalle Street. Taller windows in the south wall faced an alley separating the Stock Exchange from an adjacent, tall structure. The north wall contained the entrance and the large slate-boards where trading activities were recorded. Beneath the three-foot diameter clock stood the paneled officers' rostrum. The west wall was divided into two stories: the lower level held offices, meeting rooms, toilets, telegraph facilities, and safes; the visitors' gallery on the upper level was reached by a staircase from the ground-floor entrance hall.

During the tenancy of the Stock Exchange, the rostrum was the focal point of the room, allowing the presiding officer and secretary to direct the trading activities. It was one of the few furniture designs known to have been designed by the firm of Adler and Sullivan. The rostrum was made by Brunswick-Balke-Collender, a company with a long association to the architects, its factory at Orleans, Huron, Sedgwick, and Superior streets having been designed in stages by Adler and Sullivan between 1881 and 1893. (This landmark was destroyed by fire in April 1989.)

29. Elevation drawings of the Trading Room (prepared by the office of Vinci-Kenny Architects).

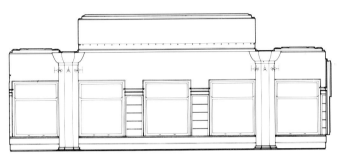

WEST ELEVATION

EAST ELEVATION

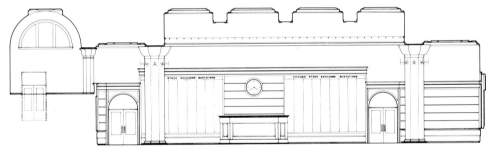

NORTH ELEVATION

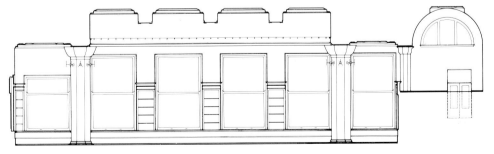

SOUTH ELEVATION

33

30. Interior view toward the tellers' windows of the National Farmers Bank (1906–08), Owatonna, Minnesota. Owatonna was the first and largest of the midwestern banks Sullivan designed late in his career. Its spatial scheme and stenciling reveal a further development of ideas expressed in the Trading Room.

Just as certain structural and interior features of the Trading Room can be traced to earlier spaces, so can a further development of its organization and decoration be found in the small banks Sullivan was to design for progressive bankers in midwestern towns after his partnership with Dankmar Adler dissolved. The National Farmers Bank (1906–08) in Owatonna, Minnesota, the first and largest of these, has a spacious banking floor, is naturally lit on two sides, and is decorated with polychromed stencils (fig. 30). While less spectacular in its spatial dimensions, the small, first-floor interior of the Home Building Association (1914) in Newark, Ohio, boldly expresses the same ornamental vocabulary. The ceiling surface is rhythmically articulated with beams, and its ornament incorporates air grilles, which, like those of the Trading Room, are proportionally spaced alongside the room's stencils (fig. 31).

The Chicago Stock Exchange Trading Room served its original function for only fourteen years, and went through at least three transformations and much decay before the building was demolished in 1972. With the perspective of the years since its restoration at the Art Institute, the long-overlooked room can now be recognized as both the notable aesthetic achievement it was in its day, and as one of many successful experiments in Louis Sullivan's forty-one-year career.

31. Interior view of the Home Building Association (1914), Newark, Ohio. The ornamental vocabulary that Sullivan used to grand effect in the Trading Room was translated to the much smaller interior of this bank, completed ten years before the architect's death.

32. Stencil on the face of the main ceiling trusses of the Trading Room (see fig. 20, no. 2). Fifty-two colors were applied to the canvas.

During the nineteenth century, one of the most popular methods of decorating interior surfaces, furniture, and small objects was the ancient technique of stenciling. Voids were cut in a flexible, impervious material (usually sheets of heavy, treated paper), and paint was forced through the openings with a stiff, short-bristled brush.

The technique interested Sullivan. He employed it in his first commissions (the "frescoing" of the Moody Tabernacle and the Sinai Temple, both completed in 1876 and now demolished), and he developed it to unparalleled richness in the Trading Room.

The commission for the decoration of the new Moody Tabernacle had come to the twenty-year-old Sullivan through his friend John Edelmann, whose firm, Johnston and Edelmann, was the building's architect. Sullivan's contribution went beyond arbitrary decoration, instead becoming an integral part of the overall architectural composition. His approach to the designs reflected ideas current in the writings of Charles Darwin and botanist Asa Gray, and in the transcendentalist aspects of Ralph Waldo Emerson, Walt Whitman, and Henry David Thoreau.

To the Transcendentalists, nature was an important key to unlocking spiritual truths and understanding human creativity. The creative individual whose thought and emotion were free from the constraints of dogma could look to the poetry of nature for personal and social meaning. Sullivan sought to interpret nature's poetry through his architecture. In a late essay entitled "Ornament in Architecture" (1892), the mature Sullivan urged architects to think of a building's ornamentation as "a garment of poetic imagery" in which "strong, athletic, and simple forms" are clad.

The Moody stencils (fig. 33) were an early expression of this ideal and were highly praised in the press for their color and originality. A *Chicago Times* reporter wrote in 1876:

The frescoing of the tabernacle is *a gracious relief from pagan fantasies* on the one hand, and flagrant abuse and vilification of sentimental devotion on the other. The design is a chaste and elegant architectural conception, wrought out in gorgeous effects of color. The underlying idea is botanical; the anatomy of plants is geometrically treated—the structural growth is carried throughout the forms, and the leaves and the flowers are seen geometrically, that is, without perspective,—as one sees their lines when pressed in the herbarium. The vision is, for an instant, obscure; the design is so recondite and its working-out so scientific that the conception does not become fully apparent until the whole is seen at once, then the unity is obvious and the details reveal themselves in their massive harmony.

But some members of the congregation seemed to hold a different opinion. An interview with the church's founder, Dwight Moody, also appeared in the *Chicago Times.*

"Your church is about ready for occupancy, Brother Moody?"

"Yes, it is looming up finely."

"There seems to be considerable difference of opinion among the congregation as to the character of *the frescoing.*"

"It's a fine job. The artist has done his work well."

"But the principal objection seems to be that it is too 'loud.' What is your opinion?"

"I don't think so. It is peculiar, but I don't see anything out of the way in it. If I had been directing it I might have had something different, but then no doubt just as many would have objected to my style as do to this. Why that work has cost already $2,200 and it would be a shame to throw all that money away. I think the frescoing is in keeping with the rest of the building. This thing of working for and trying to please the public is an ungrateful task."

The "public" prevailed. By 1882, the stencils had been painted out.

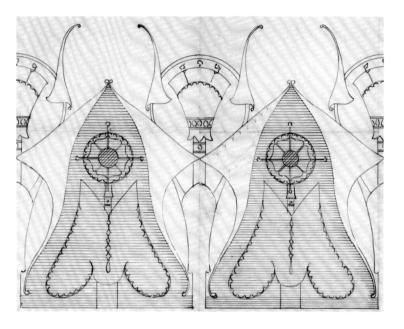

33. Louis H. Sullivan's drawing for a stencil, inscribed "Fresco border/Louis H. Sullivan to John Edelman [sic]/Paris April 1st 1875." One of Sullivan's first commissions was from Edelmann for stencils in the Moody Tabernacle (1876). The drawing reveals the rudimentary stages of Sullivan's use of organic forms, geometric repetition, and three-dimensionality in his stencil designs.

In the design of the Auditorium Building, Sullivan abandoned his earlier polychromatic color schemes and bold botanical forms for the use of elegant, gold-leafed arabesques laid over plain grounds (fig. 34). Sullivan described the scheme in a paper published in part in *Industrial Chicago* (1891):

The plastic and color decorations are distinctly architectural in conception. They are everywhere kept subordinate to the general effect of the larger structural masses and subdivisions, while lending to them the enchantment of soft tones and of varied light and shade. A single idea or principle is taken as a basis of the color scheme, that is to say, use is made of but one color in each instance, and that color is associated with gold. The color selected varies with each room treated, but the plan of using one color with gold is in no case departed from.

Polychromed stencils of up to five colors were used later in the Schiller Theater (1890–92). These designs (fig. 35), in tones of salmon, green, gold, yellow, and red, had long been painted over, and were discovered only when the theater was being demolished in 1961. Under the direction of architect Crombie Taylor, the stencil patterns were uncovered and recorded.

34. Tracing from an original stencil used above the orchestra in the Auditorium Theater (1886–90). Unlike the polychromatic scheme for the Moody Tabernacle stencils— which some members of the public found "too loud"—the Auditorium stencils used gold only, with wall colors differing by room.

35. *Tracing from an original stencil used in the Schiller Theater (1890–92). The long-forgotton polychromatic stencils were uncovered in 1961 during the theater's demolition.*

36. *Detail of Louis H. Sullivan's drawing for a stencil border in the St. Nicholas Hotel, St. Louis. The hotel (now demolished) was completed in 1895, the year after the Stock Exchange Building.*

37. Stencil on the
bottom of the upper
ceiling beams (see fig.
20, no. 4). Twenty-
one colors were
applied to the canvas.

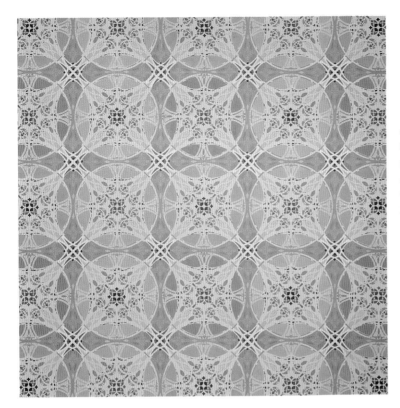

*38. Stencil on
the ceiling coffers
(see fig. 20, no. 3).
Sixteen colors
were applied
to the canvas.*

*39. Stencil on
the bottom of beam
between the Trading
Room and gallery
(see fig. 20, no.1).
Eight colors
were applied
to the canvas.*

The Trading Room stencils (figs. 32, 37–42), though unsurpassed in their richness and complexity, reflect, in their harmony with the room as a whole, Sullivan's views on the interrelationship of ornament and structure. In "Ornament in Architecture" (1892), he wrote:

It must be manifest that an ornamental design will be more beautiful if it seems a part of the surface or substance that receives it than if it looks "stuck on," so to speak. A little observation will lead one to see that in the former case there exists a peculiar sympathy between the ornament and the structure, which is absent in the latter. Both structure and ornament obviously benefit by this sympathy; each enhancing the value of the other. And this, I take it, is the preparatory basis of what may be called an organic system of ornamentation.

The ornament, as a matter of fact, is applied in the sense of being cut in or cut on, or otherwise done: yet it should appear, when completed, as though by the outworking of some beneficent agency it had come forth from the very substance of the material and was there by the same right that a flower appears amid the leaves of its parent plant.

Sullivan was to use stenciling in his later commissions as well. Noteworthy examples occur in the National Farmers Bank (1906–08) in Owatonna, Minnesota (fig. 30) and the Home Building Association Bank (1914) in Newark, Ohio (fig. 31).

40. Stencil on the north, east, and south walls above the paneling (see fig. 20, no. 7). Twenty-eight colors were applied to the canvas.

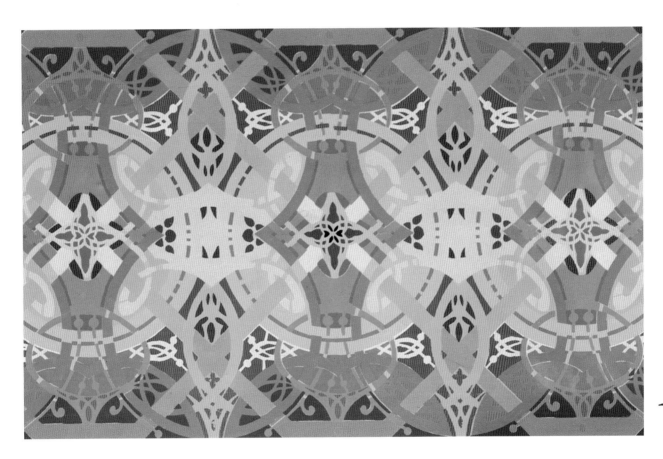

41. *Stencil on the face of the upper ceiling beams (see fig. 20, no. 5). Nineteen colors were applied to the canvas.*

42. Stencil on the bottom of the main ceiling trusses (see fig. 20, no. 6). Twenty-four colors were applied to the canvas.

In a letter of April 1, 1908, to his client Carl K. Bennett, vice president of the National Farmers Bank, Sullivan confided his fascination with the effects of color.

This is to let you know that I arrived right side up and ok; after a 5 o'clock adventure studying the color effects of the lovely grass, of very early skies, as seen along the valley of the Illinois River. My whole Spring is wrapped up just now in the study of color and out of doors for the sake of your bank decorations—which I wish to make out of doors-in-doors if I can. I am not sure that I can, but I am going to try. I am almost abnormally sensitive to color just now and every shade and nuance produces upon me an effect that is orchestral and patently sensitive to all the instruments. I know in my own mind what I am trying to achieve for you and I have in [Louis J.] Millet the best chorus master that could be found. I want a color symphony and I am pretty sure I am going to get it. I want something with many shades of the strings and the woodwinds and the brass, and I am pretty sure I am going to get it. There never has been in my entire career such an opportunity for a color tone poem as your bank interior plainly puts before me. It is not half so much a matter as to whether Millet is equal to it as whether I am equal to giving him the sufficiently delicate initiatives. I don't think I can possibly impress upon you how deep a hold this color symphony has taken upon me. And what I have in mind to accomplish—if accomplish I can. Suffice it to say that Millet is the greatest of colorists extant, and suffice further to say that I am wrapped up in your project to a degree that would be absurd in connection with anyone but yourself.

But it is unlikely that the degree of enthusiasm expressed in Sullivan's letter was restricted to the ornament for the National Farmers Bank. In the context of Sullivan's career, the stenciling for the Trading Room, executed fourteen years earlier (also with Louis J. Millet), was more than simply the decoration of a commercial space; it was one expression of an individual artistic vision that continued to grow throughout his life. Sullivan was one of the few men in the history of architecture to develop an entire system of ornament in a personal and instantly recognizable style. His accomplishment was acclaimed by his contemporaries, and as the buildings he designed have been destroyed, fragments of his ornament have become artifacts of museum value.

43. *View of LaSalle Street and the Chicago Stock Exchange Building from the northeast, c. 1965. The Washington Street arch and street-level piers have been removed and replaced with continuous store windows. A patchwork of temporary repairs is visible on the building's terracotta facade, which had blackened over the years.*

After the decision was made by The Art Institute of Chicago to reconstruct the Trading Room, documenting the room before the building's demolition became an immediate priority. The space had been repeatedly altered, and the task of determining its original condition would have to be undertaken before the remaining evidence was lost.

When the demolition began in 1971, the existence of the great Trading Room had been all but forgotten. Few photographs were taken of it during the fourteen years it had served its original function, and it was often overlooked by architectural historians. Research indicated that in 1908 the Stock Exchange organization's rent-free lease expired; because of their wish to be nearer to the south end of LaSalle Street and the Chicago Board of Trade, they moved to Burnham and Root's Rookery Building, 209 South LaSalle.

Wrecking the Building and Salvaging the Room

That same year, the Foreman Brothers' Banking Company moved into the Trading Room space. Foreman Brothers' hired the firm of Frost and Granger to remodel the Trading Room. The firm specialized in building railroad stations, and examples of their work were prevalent in Chicago and throughout the Midwest. Photographs of the remodeled room (figs. 44, 45) were discovered during the demolition among the archives of the McCormick estate, which in later years were stored in the Trading Room gallery. These photographs were salvaged before the archives were lost with the demolition of the building. The remodeling muted the original color scheme and blocked the natural illumination of the skylights. The bottom portion of stencil above the room's paneling (fig. 40) was painted out, and chandeliers were suspended from the ceiling coffers. Tennessee pink marble was added for the floors and around the newly installed tellers' cages and customer counters. The counters replaced the stock exchange officers' rostrum, which was presumably destroyed upon removal. In 1929, Foreman Brothers' was planning to move into a thirty-eight-story building it was erecting across the street. (Construction on the site is visible in fig. 4.) When the stock market crashed that year, the overextended bank failed, and the Trading Room was abandoned.

44. (left), 45. (above) Photographs of the Trading Room when it was remodeled as the Foreman Brothers' Banking Company, c. 1908–23. The most prominent changes are the addition of counters, tellers' windows, and chandeliers, the over-painting of stencil above the paneling, and the partition of the gallery. These photographs were in the archives that were later stored in the Trading Room gallery (see fig. 47), and were discovered prior to demolition.

46. *View above the false ceiling and air ducts added when the Trading Room was leased by Bell Savings and Loan in the late 1930s. The resulting concealment of the upper half of the room's ornament preserved much of it until salvage began thirty-one years later.*

47. *A column capital in the Trading Room gallery when the space was used for archive storage, 1971.*

The space was not occupied again until the late 1930s, when Bell Savings and Loan rented the room. The installation of air conditioning required the construction of a suspended ceiling (fig. 46). The mahogany wainscoting was removed and the floor area subdivided. Ironically, this misuse of the great space protected the ornament in the upper half of the room until the salvage operation began, nearly forty years later.

The final tenant in the space was the U.S.O., which operated a social center for military personnel until the building was vacated.

Demolition of the Stock Exchange had already started before the dismantling of the Trading Room was permitted to begin. Because of the public interest and protest generated by the destruction of the building, the value of its fragments was undeniable, but questions remained about how and what to salvage, and about proprietary rights to the fragments.

49, 50. Two editorial cartoons from the Chicago Sun-Times, 1971.

"IF IT WEREN'T FOR US THE CITY WOULD BE CLUTTERED WITH 'ARCHITECTURAL MASTERPIECES'"

PROGRESS?

Customarily, the wrecking company contracted to clear a demolition site retains ownership of the salvaged materials. Even as the City of Chicago, the Art Institute, and other institutions were requesting various fragments and seeking funds for their preservation, a shop had been set up in an empty storefront of the building to sell pieces of salvage as they were removed. Newspaper advertisements appeared for "Louis Sullivan Artifacts." And during the Christmas season following the demolition, paperweights made of lucite-encased chips from the terracotta facade could be ordered through a magazine ad with the headline "Jingle Bell Rock."

New obstacles presented themselves, but by November 8, 1971, the process of dismantling the room had begun. Two weeks were required to strip the false ceiling and partitions added in the late 1930s and to uncover the blocked windows and open up the gallery to the main room. This briefly "restored" the room to its original shape. The Art Institute commissioned Perry Borchers of Ohio State University to make photometric drawings for the Historic American Buildings Survey.

53. *A section of terracotta stringcourse is removed from the building before demolition, 1971.*

54. *Salvaging the Trading Room after the debris from the false ceiling and partitions had been removed, 1971.*

It was discovered that many of the original art-glass skylights, though painted or boarded over, were still in place (fig. 48), and that the cast-iron mullions that framed them were demountable. When the hidden skylights were discovered, additional costs were assessed by the wrecking company, and the salvage operation ceased until the funds could be raised. Eventually, more than 400 cast-iron skylight mullions, some weighing 175 pounds, were unbolted, numbered, and stored, and, through timely gifts, more than 200 art-glass skylight panels were crated and moved to the Art Institute's storerooms.

Newspaper descriptions of the Trading Room's opening on April 30, 1894, commented that "no less than 65 colors were used to decorate the room." When the salvage operation began, many of these patterns had long been painted over, so sections were cut from all plaster moldings, borders, and wall surfaces thought to contain such designs. The overpainting was later removed and the patterns recorded. Many of the stencils had been done on canvas, which was peeled from the ceiling and rolled up. The largest such section was taken from the coffered ceiling, and measured 7 ft. 8 in. in width by 27 ft. in length. On January 31, 1972, the last fragments were moved to The Art Institute of Chicago.

55. View to the southeast of the Trading Room after the completion of the salvage operation. Demolition of the structure had already begun.

56. *Craftsmen sanding scagliola on a column during reconstruction of the Trading Room.*

A major grant from the Walter E. Heller Foundation through its president, Mrs. Edwin J. DeCosta, made the reconstruction of the Trading Room possible. As the project progressed, escalating costs made it seem that a complete reconstruction would require additional funding, and it was suggested that only a representative portion of the room be rebuilt. Happily, just as bids for reconstruction were being received, the Walter E. Heller Foundation generously increased its grant and the complete realization of the project was assured. Funds from the Heller grant also made possible reassembly of the LaSalle Street entrance arch on Monroe Street, adjacent to the Art Institute's Columbus Drive entrance.

The Trading Room was to be placed within the museum's new East Wing, on direct axis with McKinlock Court and the Michigan Avenue entrance (fig. 57). Vinci-Kenny, the architects for the reconstruction, urged that the room be placed in its original orientation and provided with natural illumination through skylights and east windows.

Reconstruction of the Trading Room

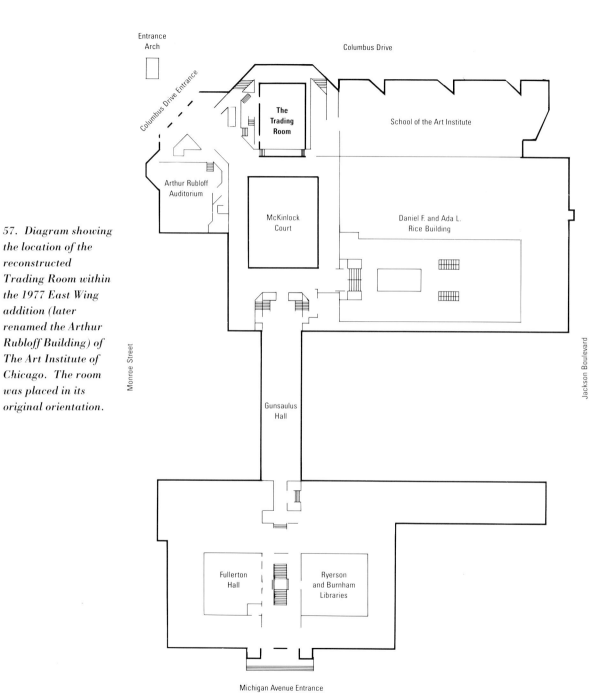

Columbus Drive

Columbus Drive Entrance

The
Trading
Room

School of the Art Institute

Arthur Rubloff
Auditorium

McKinlock
Court

Daniel F. and Ada L.
Rice Building

Monroe Street

Jackson Boulevard

Gunsaulus
Hall

Fullerton
Hall

Ryerson
and Burnham
Libraries

Michigan Avenue Entrance

57. Diagram showing the location of the reconstructed Trading Room within the 1977 East Wing addition (later renamed the Arthur Rubloff Building) of The Art Institute of Chicago. The room was placed in its original orientation.

58. The salvaged LaSalle Street entrance arch of the Chicago Stock Exchange Building as installed in the Art Institute's East Garden, adjacent to the Columbus Drive entrance, 1977. The installation was designed by the firm of Skidmore, Owings and Merrill.

Since the LaSalle Street site of the building was not in square, the east wall of the Trading Room was fifteen inches longer than the west. Project designer Walter Netsch of Skidmore, Owings and Merrill, architects for the Art Institute's East Wing, accommodated this condition by placing a slightly tapering corridor behind the room's south wall.

On March 31, 1976, the reconstruction began within the concrete-block shell. The space was scaffolded, and lathers and plasterers began to build up the beamed ceiling, which now contains the brilliant stencils (fig. 59). Templates were used to reproduce the heavy plaster moldings, some two inches in radius: an operation done with such skill that tolerances were within a fraction of an inch.

Enough sections had been salvaged of the plaster frieze carrying the initials of the Chicago Stock Exchange to permit installation of entirely original units along the south and west faces of the truss beams. New plaster units were copied for the two remaining sides (see fig. 59). Two capitals from the massive octagonal columns existed; these were installed in the southeast and southwest corners, and reproductions were made for the two northern column capitals. Only fragments of the gallery column capitals had survived, but a typical element was repaired to make the mold from which all four new capitals were cast. Where the original gold leaf of the capitals remained it was retouched; new leaf was applied to the reproductions.

Due to the brittle quality of the scagliola sheathing that had survived on two of the columns, only fragments could be salvaged for use in matching the color and mottling of a new finish. The technique of making scagliola has almost been lost in the United States, but the plaster contractors, after much investigation, located Jay Gould, an artisan in California who understood the process. Gould and two assistants were hired to recreate the sheathing of the eight columns (fig. 56). The scale and unique shape of the columns required extensive experimentation to achieve a homogeneous, monolithic appearance.

Ninety percent of the cast-iron mullions supporting the art-glass skylights had been salvaged, and missing sections were cast in aluminum. Replacing twenty-five percent of the glass was a difficult project. Colors and textures could not be matched from existing commercial supplies, and glass had to be made to order, which delayed deliveries by as much as a year.

The original ventilation grilles had been cast in plaster and permanently set into the ceiling. New, removable grilles, cast in aluminum (fig. 62), conceal the ducts which now provide both heating and air conditioning in the new room. The moldings around the bases of the columns, known from original plans to have been cast iron, had long been removed. They were redesigned from photographs, then cast in aluminum. Ductile iron was used for the stair balusters and newel posts, and given the same electroplated finish as the originals.

It was determined that the original hardware (such as doorknobs, window pulls, and push-plates) had a Bower-Barff finish, a rust-resistant coating commonly specified by Adler and Sullivan. This finish, named for its two developers, was produced by heating the hardware to 1700 degrees Fahrenheit, then injecting steam and volatile hydrocarbon liquids into the furnace to cause the deposit on the metal of a hard, nonporous, blue-black surface. Unfortunately, the finish was no longer available, and all new hardware was cast in bronze and finished to match the original Bower-Barff treatment.

60. View from the gallery of the Trading Room prior to installation of the skylights and before application of scagliola to the columns. The column capitals pictured were reproduced from the two surviving ones, which were restored and installed atop the columns to the south.

61. A painter recreates one of the room's stencils. After careful study of surviving fragments, each of fifteen different stencils was broken down into its numerous components and colors, and each shade individually applied to canvas.

The original window frames and wainscoting were of mahogany. A section of the window frame had been salvaged, but as the wainscoting had been removed thirty years earlier, its placement and detailing had to be painstakingly determined from old photographs. Honduras mahogany was used to replace both frames and wainscoting; red oak was used for the floor.

The richness and complexity of the stencils make them the most impressive single feature of the room. When the reconstruction project began, it was originally intended to reuse all of the salvaged stencils, and Robert Furhoff was hired to clean and repair them. Missing sections of stencils on canvas needed to be reproduced, as did all stencils that had originally been applied directly to plaster, and Furhoff prepared the drawings and color schedules required. Each of the fifteen different stencils had to be broken down into its numerous components and individual colors. Their geometry was reconstructed by Furhoff so as not to arbitrarily determine their center points. An analysis of the stencil used on the interior faces of the main trusses revealed the presence of fifty-two colors; thirty-one of these were found, in their original condition, on a three-inch strip of the stencil that had been overlapped during the original installation, and thus protected from light and air. The bottom portion that in 1908 had been painted out of the wall stencil (fig. 40) was uncovered, recorded, and recreated.

62. New, removable ventilation grilles are cast in aluminum. The original grilles were of plaster, and were set permanently into the Trading Room ceiling.

Furhoff supervised the reproduction of the stencils by working with the painting contractor's staff of stencil cutters and artisans as they interpreted his drawings. Natural rather than synthetic pigments were used in a zinc and oil base, and for ease of installation all the patterns were put on canvas (fig. 61). The results were so satisfactory that it was decided to use original stencil work only in the ceiling bay at the west end of the room.

Because of cost restrictions, it was not possible at the time of the reconstruction to duplicate the mahogany officers' rostrum, which was removed during the 1908 remodeling. The rostrum was an integral part of the Trading Room's composition, both functionally and visually. Fortunately, a number of old photographs, newspaper sketches, and architectural drawings documenting the rostrum survived, making its reconstruction possible in 1981 (fig. 64).

With the exception of the rostrum and the missing art glass, the Trading Room was recreated in eleven months. Throughout the process of reconstruction, tremendous pride of workmanship was exhibited by all trades.

63. *View to the east from the gallery of the reconstructed Trading Room. A striking feature of the room is visible in the different heights of windows on the east and south walls. The main column capitals to the south survive from the original room.*

*64. View to the
northeast of the
reconstructed Trading
Room showing the
officers' rostrum,
which was recon-
structed in 1981.*

*65. View to the
northeast from
the gallery of
the reconstructed
Trading Room.*

Adler
and
Sullivan

66. (above)
Dankmar Adler in
1889 at age 45.

67. (above, right)
Louis H. Sullivan in
1900 at age 44.

Dankmar Adler, 1844–1900

Dankmar Adler was born on July 3, 1844, in Lengsfeld, Germany, near Eisenach. He came to America with his father, Liebman, in 1854, and they settled in Detroit, where his father became a rabbi and cantor. Dankmar's interest in architectural drawing led his father to apprentice him to an architect in Detroit. In May 1861, the Adler family moved to Chicago. Ten years later Adler formed a partnership with Edward Burling, but after carrying most of the work load in the partnership, he established an independent practice in 1879.

His first independent project, the Central Music Hall, stood at the corner of Randolph and State streets until 1901, and was the prototype for a number of theaters he and his partner Louis Sullivan designed in later years. It was Adler's intuitive grasp of acoustic principles that determined the layout of the orchestra, balconies, and ceiling coves in these theaters, which included the Auditorium, McVickers, and Schiller theaters.

Louis H. Sullivan, 1856–1924

Louis Sullivan was born in Boston in 1856. Throughout his education, Sullivan was deeply impressed by the innovative scientific, philosophical, and artistic movements of his time, and he later adapted their precepts to develop a personal architectural style based on the concept of man as a creative being within the context of nature. In 1872, Sullivan entered the architectural school at the Massachusetts Institute of Technology, but left after one year with the intent of studying at the Ecole des Beaux-Arts in Paris. Instead, he worked in the office of Frank Furness in Philadelphia, but the panic of 1873 forced him to leave after a short time.

Since his parents had moved to Chicago four years earlier, Sullivan decided to visit them. Appalled by the ruin left in the wake of the 1871 Chicago Fire, yet excited by the prospect of rebuilding, Sullivan took a job as a draftsman with Major William Le Baron Jenney. There he met John Edelmann, who shared his interest in organically based ornamentation, and who would later introduce him to Dankmar Adler. Within a year, Sullivan left Chicago for Paris and the Ecole des Beaux-Arts, but returned within a year as draftsman and designer for various firms. In 1880, he worked for Dankmar Adler; their partnership was formed in 1883. After the partnership dissolved in 1895, Sullivan's career reached its pinnacle with his design for the Schlesinger and Mayer Store (now Carson Pirie Scott, 1898–99, 1902–03), southeast corner of State and Madison. The completion of this seminal project was followed by a period of personal and financial troubles that caused his career to wane. It was revived for a time through the patronage of progressive bankers in midwestern towns, but in his last years Sullivan was destitute. He published *The Autobiography of an Idea* and *A System of Architectural Ornament According with a Philosophy of Man's Powers* in 1924, the year he died.

The Partnership of Adler and Sullivan, 1883–1895

The firm of Adler and Sullivan executed more than 200 projects, including over 100 residences, many stores, warehouses, office buildings, tombs, synagogues, hotels, and theaters. Among the most prominent examples of their work in Chicago were the Auditorium Building (1886–90), the Ryerson Tomb (1889), the Getty Tomb (1890), the Schiller Theater Building (1890–92), the Charnley House (1891), the Transportation Building (1891–93), and the Chicago Stock Exchange Building (1893–94); and, outside of Chicago, the Wainwright Building (1890–92) in St. Louis and the Guaranty Building (1894–96) in Buffalo. The Chicago Stock Exchange Building was one of the last major buildings designed by Adler and Sullivan before their partnership was dissolved in 1895. Among the employees of Adler and Sullivan at the time of the Chicago Stock Exchange Building commission was Frank Lloyd Wright, who resigned his position as chief draftsman soon after construction commenced in 1893. Wright was succeeded in the firm by George Grant Elmslie, who continued to work with Sullivan until 1909.

Architects and Contractors

Bibliography

The Chicago Stock Exchange Building, 1893–94

Architects:
Adler and Sullivan

Civil engineer:
William Sooy Smith

Contractor:
Victor Falkenau and Brothers

Stained glass and frescoing:
Healy and Millet

Masons:
Chicago Hydraulic Pressed Brick Company

Ornamental iron:
The Winslow Brothers Company

Wood finishing:
Brunswick-Balke-Collender Company

Plate glass, mirrors, and beveled glass:
James H. Rice Company

Prismatic skylights:
Brown Brothers Manufacturing Company

Gas and electrical fixtures:
Alexander H. Revell and Company

Hardware trimmings:
Orr and Lockett Hardware Company

Furniture:
J. S. Ford, Johnson and Company

Terracotta:
The Northwestern Terra Cotta Works of Chicago

Fireproofing:
Pioneer Fire Proof Construction Company

Heating and ventilating system:
Andrew Johnson Company

Plumbing:
T. W. Potts and Company

Reconstruction of the Trading Room and the Stock Exchange Arch, 1976–77

Architects for the reconstruction:
Vinci-Kenny, Architects

Structural and mechanical engineers:
Skidmore, Owings and Merrill

General contractor for the reconstruction:
Reed Illinois Corporation

Painting and decorating:
Nelson-Sholin Painting Company

Plastering and lathing:
Reed Illinois Corporation

Metalwork:
Custom Architectural Metals, Inc.

Millwork:
Hartmann-Sanders Company

Art glass:
Wenz Art Glass

Glazing:
Tyler and Hippach Glass Company

Sconces and clock:
New Metal Crafts, Inc.

Marble and Slate:
McCue Marble Corporation

Hardware:
Clark and Barlow Hardware Company

Floor:
Johnson Floor Company, Inc.

Electrical work:
Kil-Bar Electric Company

Architects for the Centennial Project:
Skidmore, Owings and Merrill, Walter A. Netsch, principal in charge of design

General Contractors for the Centennial Project:
Morse/Diesel, Inc.

Architects for the reconstruction of the arch:
Skidmore, Owings and Merrill

General contractors and masons:
Crouch-Walker Corporation

Terracotta suppliers:
Gladding, McBean and Co.

Selected Primary Sources and Reviews

"Art Themes." *Chicago Times.* May 21, 1876, 2.

"Chicago Stock Exchange Building." *Daily Inter Ocean* (Chicago). February 26, 1893, 24.

"Chicago Stock Exchange Building, Chicago." *Ornamental Iron II.* Winslow Bros. Co. Ornamental Iron Works. July 1894, 7–13.

"Exchange in a New Home." *Chicago Daily News.* April 30, 1894, 2.

"For Bulls and Bears." *Chicago Times.* May 1, 1894, 7.

Fleming, I. A. *Chicago Stock Exchange.* Chicago: I. A. Fleming, 1894.

"Hegira of Brokers." *Chicago Evening Journal,* April 30, 1894, 1.

Industrial Chicago: The Building Interests, Vol. I. Chicago: Goodspeed Publishing Company, 1891.

"Nearing Completion." *Chicago Evening Journal.* April 23, 1894, 54.

"New Mart of Finance." *Chicago Herald.* May 1, 1894, 4.

"New Palace of Trade." *Chicago Record.* April 28, 1894, 3.

"Opened for Trading." *Daily Inter Ocean* (Chicago). May 1, 1894, 7.

Schuyler, Montgomery. "A critique (with illustrations) of the works of Adler and Sullivan, D. H. Burnham & Co., Henry Ives Cobb" Great American Architects' Series, no. 2. New York: *Architectural Record,* December, 1895.

"Stock Exchange Open." *The Chicago Record.* May 1, 1894, 2.

Sullivan, Louis H. "The Autobiography of an Idea." *Journal of the American Institute of Architects* (June 1922–July 1923). Reprint. New York: Dover, 1956.

——. "Development of Building II." *The Economist* 56 (July 1916), 39–40.

——. *Kindergarten Chats and Other Writings.* New York: George Wittenborn, Inc., 1947.

——. "The Tall Office Building Artistically Considered." Lippincott's 57 (March 1896), 403–9. Reprinted in Sullivan, *Kindergarten Chats*, 1947.

"Temple of Finance." *Chicago Evening Post.* April 30, 1894, 1–2.

"The Saint's Rest–Brother Moody . . . What He Thinks of the Frescoing of the New Tabernacle. . . ." *Chicago Times.* May 31, 1876, 3.

"Temple for Brokers." *Chicago Evening Journal.* April 28, 1894, 5.

"Warming the House." *Chicago Tribune.* May 1, 1894, 12.

Selected Later Sources

Andrew, David S. *Louis Sullivan and the Polemics of Modern Architecture.* Urbana: University of Illinois Press, 1985.

Bush-Brown, Albert. *Louis Sullivan.* New York: George Braziller, 1960.

Bruegmann, Robert, Donald Hoffman, Edward Kaufman, Gerald Larson, Pauline Saliga, and Lauren Weingarden. *Fragments of Chicago's Past.* Chicago: The Art Institute of Chicago (forthcoming, 1989).

Condit, Carl. *The Chicago School of Architecture.* Chicago: University of Chicago Press, 1964.

Connely, Willard. *Louis Sullivan as He Lived: The Shaping of American Architecture.* New York: Horizon Press, 1960.

Hanks, David. "Louis J. Millet and The Art Institute of Chicago." *Bulletin of The Art Institute of Chicago* 67 (March–April, 1973), 13–19.

Kaufmann, Edgar, Jr., ed. *Louis Sullivan and the Architecture of Free Enterprise.* Chicago: The Art Institute of Chicago, 1956.

Menocal, Narciso G. *Architecture as Nature: The Transcendentalist Idea of Louis Sullivan.* Madison: University of Wisconsin Press, 1981.

Millett, Larry. *The Curve of the Arch: The Story of Louis Sullivan's Owatonna Bank.* St. Paul: Minnesota Historical Society, 1985.

Morrison, Hugh. *Louis Sullivan: Prophet of Modern Architecture.* New York: Museum of Modern Art and Norton, 1935.

Perlman, Daniel H. *The Auditorium Building: Its History and Architectural Significance.* Chicago: Roosevelt University, 1976.

Pollak, Martha. "Sullivan and the Orders of Architecture." *Chicago Architecture, 1872–1922: Birth of a Metropolis,* 251–65. Ed. John Zukowsky. Munich and Chicago: Prestel Verlag and The Art Institute of Chicago, 1987.

Randall, Frank A. *History of the Development of Building Construction in Chicago.* Urbana: University of Illinois, 1949.

Rice, Wallace. *The Chicago Stock Exchange: A History.* Chicago: The Committee on Library of the Chicago Stock Exchange, 1923.

Southern Illinois University at Edwardsville. *Louis H. Sullivan Architectural Ornament Collection.* Edwardsville: S.I.U.E., 1981.

Sprague, Paul E., ed. *The Drawings of Louis Henry Sullivan: A Catalogue of the Frank Lloyd Wright Collection at the Avery Architectural Library.* Princeton, N.J.: Princeton University Press, 1979.

Szarkowski, John. *The Idea of Louis Sullivan.* Minneapolis: University of Minnesota Press, 1956.

Twombly, Robert C. *Louis Sullivan: His Life and Work.* New York: Viking, 1986.

——, ed. *Louis Sullivan: The Public Papers.* Chicago and London: University of Chicago Press, 1988.

Underhill, Sarah M., ed. *Louis Sullivan in The Art Institute of Chicago: A Catalogue of the Collections.* New York: Garland, 1989.

Vinci, John. "The Chicago Stock Exchange Building." *Chicago History* 3 (Spring–Summer 1974), 23–27.

Warn, Robert R. "Part I: Bennett & Sullivan, Client & Creator." *Prairie School Review* 10 (Third Quarter, 1973), 5–15.

de Wit, Wim, ed. *Louis Sullivan: The Function of Ornament.* New York and London: Norton, 1986.

Weingarden, Lauren S. *Louis H. Sullivan: The Banks, 1906–1920.* Cambridge, Mass.: MIT Press, 1987.

——. "Louis H. Sullivan's Ornament and the Poetics of Architecture." *Chicago Architecture, 1872–1922: Birth of a Metropolis,* 229–49. Ed. John Zukowsky. Munich and Chicago: Prestel Verlag and The Art Institute of Chicago, 1987.

Wright, Frank Lloyd. *Genius and the Mobocracy.* Enlarged edition. New York: Horizon Press, 1971.

The Art Institute of Chicago, 1988–89

Credits

Most of the historic photographs contained herein are from the archives of the Ryerson and Burnham Libraries at The Art Institute of Chicago. Unless otherwise listed below, all photographs, including reproductions of archival material, are by the Department of Photographic Services, The Art Institute of Chicago, Alan Newman, Executive Director.

Richard Nickel: 5, 6, 10, 11, 12, 16, 17, 18, 26, 43, 46, 47, 48, 51, 52, 54, 55. Hedrich Blessing: cover stencil, 32, 37, 38, 39, 40, 41, 42. Bob Thall: front cover (inset), 25, 63, 64, 65. Barbara Crane: 58. John Vinci: 56, 59, 60, 61, 62. Michael J. Pado: 3. Figures 14 and 15: *Ornamental Iron II* (July 1894), Winslow Bros. Co. Ornamental Iron Works, Chicago; courtesy of Tim Samuelson. Frontispiece: Courtesy of Powell's Bookstore, Hyde Park. Fig. 1: *Harper's Weekly Magazine,* Jan. 12, 1895. Figs. 2, 13, 33, 36: Avery Architectural and Fine Arts Library, Columbia University in the City of New York. Figs. 49, 50: cartoons by Jacob Burck, courtesy of W. R. Hasbrouck; reproduced with permission of the *Chicago Sun-Times.* Figs. 20, 21, 22, 23, 24, 29: office of John Vinci. Figs. 34, 35: Crombie Taylor Associates.